ONLINE BUSINESS GAME PLAN

A 21-Day Game Plan To Launch Your Online Business

Dan Frigo

Table of Contents

Introduction	5
Day One: Choose A Profitable Niche	8
Day Two: Set Goals	15
Day Three: Choose A Domain	21
Day Four: Get Hosting	27
Day Five: Install WordPress	30
Day Six: Set Up WordPress	35
Day Seven: Choose A Website Theme/Design	44
Day Eight: Create A Logo	47
Day Nine: Create Foundational Pages Content	51
Day Ten: Set Up Your Blog	57
Day Eleven: Create A Free Giveaway	63
Day Twelve: Set Up An Autoresponder	67
Day Thirteen: Set Up Your Lead Capture Page	75
Day Fourteen: Create Your Thank You Page	80
Day Fifteen: Choose Your Core Offer	83
Day Sixteen: Set Up Your Core Offer Sales Engine	87

Day Seventeen: Write Your Email Campaign	93
Day Eighteen: Choose Your Authority Platform	97
Day Nineteen: Create Your Content Base	99
Day Twenty: Set Up Pixels And A Tracking System	102
Day Twenty-One: Set Up Your Backend Funnel	107
Final Words	109

© Copyright 2019 Dan Frigo - All rights reserved.

No part of this material may be used, reproduced, distributed or transmitted in any form and by any means whatsoever, including without limitation photocopying, recording or other electronic or mechanical methods or by any information storage and retrieval system, without the prior written permission from the author, except for brief excepts in a review.

This book is intended to provide general information on business only. Neither the author nor publisher provide any legal or other professional advice. If you need professional advice, you should seek advice from the appropriate licensed professional. This book does not provide complete information on the subject matter covered. This book is not intended to address specific requirements, either for an individual or an organization. This book is intended to be used only as a general guide, and not as a sole source of information on the subject matter. While the author has undertaken diligent efforts to ensure accuracy, there is no guarantee of accuracy or of no errors, omissions or typographical errors. Any slights of people or organizations are unintentional. Any reference to any person or organization whether living or dead is purely coincidental. The author and publisher shall have no liability or responsibility to any person or entity and hereby disclaim all liability, including without limitation, liability for consequential damages regarding any claim, loss or damage that may be incurred, or alleged to have been incurred, directly or indirectly, arising out of the information provided in this book.

Introduction

Welcome to *Online Business Game Plan: A 21-Day Game Plan To Launch Your Online Business!* This proven game plan will help you kick off a successful online business in less than a month.

Over the next 21 days, you will learn everything you need to lay the foundation for a successful online business. All you need to do to set yourself up to earn big is follow the steps within this book.

By the time you finish this course, you will have:

- Goals and targets set up to keep you on track.

- Your live website ready to welcome paying customers.

- A core offer and a system in place to promote it.

- An email campaign in place to establish trust with your potential customers and convert leads into buyers.

- A lead capture system in place to build your email list.

- A backend offer system set up to maximize your revenue and customer long-term value.
- And everything else you need to for success in your online business!

Here is a day-by-day breakdown of what we will cover:

Day 1: Choose a profitable niche

Day 2: Set goals

Day 3: Choose a domain

Day 4: Get hosting

Day 5: Install WordPress

Day 6: Set up WordPress

Day 7: Choose a website theme and design

Day 8: Create a logo

Day 9: Create website foundational pages

Day 10: Set up your blog

Day 11: Create a free giveaway

Day 12: Set up an autoresponder

Day 13: Set up your lead capture page

Day 14: Create your thank you page

Day 15: Choose your core offer

Day 16: Set up your core offer sales engine

Day 17: Write your email campaign

Day 18: Choose your authority platform

Day 19: Create your content base

Day 20: Set up pixels and a tracking system

Day 21: Set up your backend funnel

So, let's get started!

Day One: Choose A Profitable Niche

Today, you will take the first step toward launching your online business by selecting a niche market. This step can mean all the difference between a successful online business and one that fails. Choosing a niche that you will enjoy working in is extremely important. However, it is equally important that the niche you choose has the potential to be profitable. By the end of the day, you will have selected a profitable niche market that you are excited to build your online business around.

To get started, you must identify a niche that you will enjoy. The goal is to build a business around a concept that makes you excited to get out of bed every day and go to work. Once you have identified a few niches you're interested in pursuing, you will need to analyze the profitability of each of them to determine which is the best choice.

Your Interests

Your own interests are a great place to start. Remember, you want to find a niche that you are extremely interested in; if you build your business around one of your major interests, you will approach your business with passion, which is your first step to ensuring success.

To determine some of the things you are interested in, answer the questions below:

What kind of products do you buy?

What books and magazines do you read?

What websites do you frequent?

What are some of your biggest passions?

What are some of your hobbies?

What would be a dream business for you?

Your Skills, Strengths, And Knowledge

Another good idea when deciding your niche is to catalogue your skills, strengths, and knowledge. Did your last job teach you a very specific skill set? What did you major in in college? Do you have a long-time hobby that could be considered a skill? Are you great at accounting or quilting or organizing?

Whatever it may be, list the skills, strengths, and knowledge that you already possess.

By now, you have identified a number of your interests, skills, strengths, and areas of knowledge. Take a look at the list you've made and narrow it down to your top five.

Test Profitability

There is, of course, no way to completely ensure that a niche market will make you money. However, you can do some research that will provide you with a number of indicators that a niche is successful. Basically, you want to make sure that people are passionate about and are spending money on whatever niche you decide to pursue.

A great place to start your research is a quick and easy Google search. Choose one of your top five ideas and begin searching a keyword for that idea in conjunction with terms that indicate people are spending money on the topic.

For example, say that you identified earlier that you are very skilled with spreadsheets and enjoying working with them. One of your keywords could be "Microsoft Excel." Here are a few ideas of searches you could do:

"Microsoft Excel books"

"Microsoft Excel courses"

"Microsoft Excel coaching"

"Microsoft Excel seminar"

"Microsoft Excel webinar"

Say you decide to search for "Microsoft Excel courses." This search will indicate a few positive things about this niche.

First, you will see that there are several advertisers spending money on this keyword.

Online Microsoft Excel Courses | Learn Anytime, Anywhere.
[Ad] www.linkedin.com/learning/Excel ▼
Enhance Your Excel Skills With Expert-Led Online Video Courses - Start Today! Start Your Free Month. Learn In-Demand Skills. With Lynda.com Content. Expert-Led Courses. Access Anytime, Anywhere. Courses: Process Modeling, Charts in Depth, Formulas & Functions, Formatting Techniques.

Excel 2016 Training
Stay Up To Date With Excel 2016 Essential Training. Get Started!

Excel Tips and Tricks
Learn Productivity Boosting Tricks & Shortcuts Using Microsoft Excel.

Online Microsoft Excel Courses | Interactive Excel Course
[Ad] www.exceleverest.com/ ▼
Comprehensive Excel course w/ easy to follow curriculum & interactive exercises. Learn by Doing. Track Your Progress. Money Back Guarantee. Practical Exercises. Learn At Your Own Pace. Interactive Training. For All Skill Levels. Courses: Excel Basics, Formulas, Charts, Pivot Tables.
Corporate Training · How It Works · FAQ · Contact Us

Local Excel Classes | View 2018 Class Dates & Prices | certstaff.com
[Ad] www.certstaff.com/Microsoft/Excel ▼
Microsoft Excel Training. Live Instructors Teaching. Hands-on Courses. Versions 2016/2013/10.
Courses: Excel 2016, Excel 2013, Excel 2010, Microsoft Office.
Excel 2016 - Level 1 - from $335.00 - Learn Basic Skills · More ▼

If companies are willing to spend valuable advertising dollars on a topic, it's a good bet that it's a worthwhile and profitable niche.

Next, you will see that there are courses available on this particular topic on popular course platforms like Coursera and Udemy.

Excel | edX
https://www.edx.org/learn/excel
Free **Excel courses** online. Learn **Excel** data analysis and visualization skills to advance your career with free **courses** from **Microsoft** on edX. Join now.

Microsoft Excel Courses | Coursera
https://www.coursera.org/courses?query=microsoft%20excel
Learn online and earn valuable credentials from top universities like Yale, Michigan, Stanford, and leading companies like Google and IBM. Join Coursera for ...

Microsoft Excel - From Beginner to Expert in 6 Hours | Udemy
https://www.udemy.com/thebestexcel/
May 24, 2018 - This **Microsoft Excel** class will make you a master of **Microsoft Excel**. The **training** uses **Excel** 2013 for Windows.

Microsoft Excel - Excel from Beginner to Advanced | Udemy
https://www.udemy.com/microsoft-excel-2013-from-beginner-to-advanced-and-beyo...
May 24, 2018 - Excel with this A-Z **Microsoft Excel Course**. Microsoft Excel 2010, Excel 2013, Excel 2016.

Excel - Online Courses, Classes, Training, Tutorials on Lynda
https://www.lynda.com/Excel-training-tutorials/192-0.html
Excel tutorials review pivot tables and charts with experts from lynda.com. Learn **microsoft excel training** for versions 2007, 2010 and 2013.

The willingness of large companies to invest in this topic indicates that the niche is profitable.

Do this for each of your top five niche ideas and make notes about what you find. You can customize the search terms to be most relevant to each niche. For example, you can search "cooking magazines," "weight loss products," comic book events," etc. Search for as many relevant terms as you can think of so you get the fullest picture of profitability possible.

Choose Your Niche

With your research complete, it's time to make your final decision about the niche market you will choose to target. Remember that profitability is not the only factor. Yes, your niche needs to be profitable, but the most profitable niche may not be the one that is most interesting to you.

If you find that your favorite niche is not the *most* profitable, it's okay. You want to build a business that makes you money *and* excites you. Which business idea would you be most excited to build? Spend some time going over your notes and reflecting before you decide which niche is the best choice for you.

Action Steps

- Identify your interests by asking the following questions:
    - What kind of products do you buy?
    - What books and magazines do you read?
    - What websites do you frequent?
    - What are some of your biggest passions?
    - What are some of your hobbies?
    - What would be a dream business for you?
- Make a list of the skills, strengths, and knowledge you possess.

- Narrow down your list of ideas to your top five.
- Test the profitability of your top five niches
    - Do the following relevant searches for each niche on Google:
        - "Keyword books"
        - "Keyword magazines"
        - "Keyword courses"
        - "Keyword products"
        - "Keyword coaching"
        - "Keyword seminars"
        - "Keyword webinars"
        - "Keyword events"
    - Take notes on the results of your searches so you can determine which niche is most profitable.
- Choose your niche.

Tomorrow, you will set goals and lay out targets to keep you on track and maintain forward momentum.

Day Two: Set Goals

Unfortunately, goals are often overlooked by those trying to build an online business. However, they are one of the most important parts of a successful business plan. When you create goals and targets for your online business, you create a way to measure and track the success of your business.

Today, you will learn how to set big goals and targets, and then break down those goals and targets into smaller steps. By the end of the day, you will have goals and a daily plan in place to achieve them!

Goals Should Be SMART

How to set proper goals:

Goals should be specific and measurable. This means that goals need to be tied to an end result that you can track and measure against. A great example is the goal of earning $5,000 a month. This is specific and can easily be measured.

Goals should be challenging but attainable. Don't be afraid to dream, but make sure your goals are realistic. If it's completely out of the realm of possibility, it is **NOT** a good goal. Your goals should push you to work hard but should be within reach. If you consistently set unattainable goals, you will quickly be discouraged because you don't meet them.

Goals should have purpose and meaning. Let's say that your goal is to make $5,000 a month. This goal should serve a purpose. Why do you want to make $5,000 a month? Maybe it's so you can replace your regular income and become a full-time online business owner. This gives the goal meaning.

Goals should line up with your vision. This is an important one that is easy to forget. Goals are not all about big sales figures or huge customer bases. Remember to stay true to your vision for your online business when creating goals. For example, if you want to create your fitness business to help people get in shape, your goals can be about getting a certain amount of positive feedback or number of satisfied customers rather than about income.

Goals should have deadlines. When you set your goals, you need to ensure that you set a time by which you should achieve them. For example, if you want to earn 500 loyal subscribers for your newsletter, you need to set a deadline for this. Otherwise, you will not be motivated to do the work necessary to get those 500 subscribers. You won't ever fail, so why bother rushing? Instead, you could dedicate yourself to getting 500 subscribers by the end of your first month.

Major Goals

Using these goal best practices, it's time to set a few major goals for your online business. You want to set three to seven major goals. Make sure that your goals are specific, measurable, achievable, relevant, and time-bound (SMART). These are the criteria described in the previous section. Here are a few examples of major goals you can set:

- Generate a certain number of leads
- Get a certain number of subscribers
- Generate a certain number of sales
- Generate a certain amount of income
- Generate a certain amount of traffic
- Have a certain number of satisfied customers

Smaller Goals

Major goals can feel overwhelming, especially when you've followed the advice of making them challenging (but attainable). To combat this and ensure you stay on track, you can break your major goals into smaller, more manageable chunks.

Let's say you decide to make it one of you major goals to earn $100,000 in your first year. That's doable, yes, but it's also pretty ambitious! It might even start to seem a little too daunting to you. A good idea, then, is to break this earnings figure down into quarterly and monthly figures.

So,

Yearly: $100,000

Quarterly: $25,000

Monthly: $8,333 (and some change)

You can even break it down into weekly figures if you wish. These smaller goals will keep you on track toward your ultimate goal AND they will make the major goal seem more attainable. They can also help you determine if the actions you are taking to reach your goal are effective.

Repeat this process for each of your major goals.

Plan of Action

The next step is to take action and make a plan! Too many people set goals but don't define the actions they will take to achieve those goals. Without a plan of action, goals are meaningless.

Think about each of the major goals you set and about the smaller, stepping-stone goals for each of those. What actions do you need to take to meet those goals?

Let's continue with our previous example. If you want to earn $100,000 a year, what must you do? You might need to do a certain amount of marketing or launch a specific number of new products.

It is important to remember that this process is not an exact science. As your business grows and you learn, you will be better able to understand and predict what needs to be done in order to meet your goals. However, you are really just making your best educated guess.

Make a list of actions you need to take in order to meet your major goals. You can break these actions down into more manageable steps that are in line with your smaller goals.

Daily Plan

The last part of the goal-setting process is creating a daily plan. You have broken down your goals and determined the big steps you need to take to achieve those goals. Now, you can lay out a daily plan to make sure you achieve each step and meet your goals along the way.

Let's say that we determined that to earn $100,000 in your first year, you need to update your blog with relevant content twice a week.

A daily plan for completing this action might look like this:

Monday – Come up with the week's blog topics and research

Tuesday – Research and prepare notes for both of the week's posts

Wednesday – Write and post the week's first blog post

Thursday – Write and post the week's second blog post

Friday – Promote your posts on all social media channels

Creating and sticking to this kind of plan ensures that you are working toward your goals consistently, which is vital to the success of an online business.

Action Steps

- Set three to seven major goals for your online business.
- Break those major goals down into quarterly and monthly goals.
- Make a list of the actions you need to take to achieve your goals.
- Create a daily plan.

Tomorrow, you will choose the domain name for your online business's website.

Day Three: Choose A Domain

Choosing a good domain name for your online business can be tough. However, a common mistake is getting caught up in finding the right domain name and spending too much time on this step. The information in this section will make it easier for you to find a good domain name without agonizing over the process.

By the end of the day, you will have selected the domain name that you will use for your business!

Brainstorm

There are a few different ways to come up with a good domain name for your business. The best way to start is by brainstorming a list of potential business names. These names can be combinations of words or ideas you like, niche-related, etc. Put down anything that comes to mind and let the ideas flow. At this point, the names don't have to be perfect. You just want to get a list of 25 to 50 potential names to act as a starting point and give you something to work with.

However, remember these tips when brainstorming:

- Choose something easy to remember. Think catchy!
- Shorter is better.

- Numbers can make finding the right domain confusing (Is it spelled out? Is it just the numerals?). Intentionally changing the spelling of words can also mean users have a difficult time finding the right domain.

Narrow It Down

Take your list and cross off the ones that don't sound quite right or that you're just not feeling. You want to narrow down your list to only the ones that you truly like and that you are interested in working with. Shoot for narrowing it down to your top five to 10 names.

Add Words

This is an optional step (and in fact, you may already have covered this step), but it can give you more ideas and give you access to more potentially-available domain names.

Let's say that you want to start an online business that sells handmade children's clothing. You've come up with the brand name "Cute As A Button." You could add the word "clothing" or the word "designs" to the end of this name to give you other domain name options: "Cute As A Button Clothing" or "Cute As A Button Designs."

See if you can come up with a few variations for each of your top potential names.

If you are having trouble coming up with terms to add to your names or you want to come up with more options, a great tool is https://www.leandomainsearch.com/. You can type in any keyword or words and it will append words and tell you if the domain created is available. For our "Cute As A Button" example, it yields the following results (this is only a partial list; you will notice that there are 4,993 available domains containing this phrase!):

cute as a button		SEARCH DOMAINS
Found 4,993 available domains containing "cuteasabutton" in 0.46s		
MyCuteAsAButton	CuteAsAButtonBlog	CuteAsAButtonWeb
CuteAsAButtonWorld	GoCuteAsAButton	CuteAsAButtonGroup
CuteAsAButtonMedia	TheCuteAsAButton	WebCuteAsAButton
CuteAsAButtonShop	CuteAsAButtonApp	ProCuteAsAButton
CuteAsAButtonBook	CuteAsAButtonNetwork	CuteAsAButtonInc
CuteAsAButtonNet	CuteAsAButtonNews	CuteAsAButtonSite
CuteAsAButtonTv	CuteAsAButtonNow	CuteAsAButtonCenter
NetCuteAsAButton	CuteAsAButtonPlus	AllCuteAsAButton
CuteAsAButtonPro	CuteAsAButtonLink	CuteAsAButtonClub
CuteAsAButtonMarket	CuteAsAButtonTech	SmartCuteAsAButton
FreeCuteAsAButton	EcoCuteAsAButton	CuteAsAButtonBox
DigitalCuteAsAButton	CuteAsAButtonHub	CuteAsAButtonData
GreenCuteAsAButton	CuteAsAButtonInfo	CuteAsAButtonCity
CuteAsAButtonDirect	OnlineCuteAsAButton	CuteAsAButtonCentral
CuteAsAButtonHouse	CuteAsAButtonLife	GlobalCuteAsAButton

Check Availability

Take another look at your list. You should have a couple variations on each name. Narrow this list down to your favorites. You may end up with several variations in your top five or you may end up with five totally different names. It's all up to you.

Starting with your favorite, do a domain search to see if it is available. You can find many sites on which to do this, but one of the most popular (and reputable) is https://www.godaddy.com/

To check whether your domain name is available, type your idea into the search bar, as shown:

Click "Search" to see if your domain is available. If it is, you will see this screen:

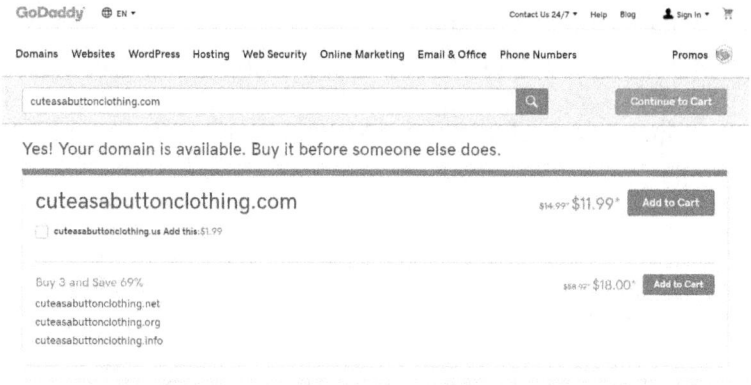

If your domain choice is NOT available, you will see a screen like this:

If your first domain choice is taken, just move onto the next one. You will notice that GoDaddy offers suggestions of domains that are available. Often, these domains will have extensions other than ".com." For best results, you should choose a domain name with a .com extension.

Once you find an available domain name that you like, buy it!

Action Steps

- Brainstorm a list of 25 to 50 potential business names.
- Narrow down your list to the top 5 to 10 that you like.
- Append niche or action words to each of these.
- Narrow down your list again to the top 5 to 10.
- Check domain name availability, starting with your favorite.
- Buy your domain name.

Tomorrow, you will secure hosting for your new domain.

Day Four: Get Hosting

Today, you will be getting hosting for your domain. Your web host, or web hosting service provider, provides the technologies needed for your website to be viewed on the internet. Basically, you can think of getting hosting as renting space on a computer to store your website files. By the time you complete today's lesson, you will have acquired hosting and attach it to your domain so that you can get your website online.

Choose A Hosting Service And Package

Most domain registrars, such as GoDaddy, also offer hosting services. The easiest option for you is to use the same site for both domain registration and hosting. With GoDaddy, for example, you can secure hosting and add your domain with just a few clicks.

Here is a screenshot of some of GoDaddy's hosting package offerings:

	Best Value		
Economy	**Deluxe**	**Ultimate**	**Business Hosting**
Go live with the essentials.	More space and flexibility for multiple sites.	Hosts complex sites, perfect for a growing business.	Optimized for high-traffic, eCommerce and resource-demanding sites.
As low as	As low as	As low as	As low as
$2.99/mo	**$4.99**/mo	**$7.99**/mo	**$20.99**/mo
On sale - Save 62%	On sale - Save 54%	On sale - Save 52%	On sale - Save 30%
$7.99/mo when you renew⁴	$10.99/mo when you renew⁴	$15.99/mo when you renew⁴	$29.99/mo when you renew⁴
Add to Cart	Add to Cart	Add to Cart	Learn More
Award-winning, 24/7 support	Economy features, plus	Deluxe features, plus	Ultimate features, plus
1 website	Unlimited websites^10	2x processing power & memory	VPS power with cPanel ease of use
Unmetered bandwidth	Unlimited storage	Free SSL Certificate - 1 year†† ($74.99 value)	Dedicated resources
New PHP 7.0, 7.1	Unlimited subdomains		Free SSL Certificate††
Free Microsoft Office 365 Business Email - 1 year ($59.88 value)		Free Premium DNS ($35.88/yr value)	
Free domain* with annual plan (up to $34.99 value)		Unlimited Databases	

When you are first starting out, you have no need for an elaborate hosting package, so don't fall into the trap of thinking you need to most expensive one with the most features. Notice in the previous screenshot that you can host a website for as little as $2.99 a month. It might be best to start this simple and upgrade later if you have the need. Just remember to look for a hosting package that at least has easy WordPress installation and cPanel access.

Connect Your Domain To Your Host

This is where it gets a little tricky. Because each hosting provider is different, the process of connecting your domain to your web host will depend on where you secure hosting. However, every provider should have tutorials for this process and many, including GoDaddy, have live chat or phone support where an expert can walk you through the process.

Action Steps

- Choose your hosting provider and hosting package.
- Connect your domain to your host.

Tomorrow, you will be installing WordPress on your domain.

Day Five: Install WordPress

It's finally time to get your website online! By the end of the day, you will have installed WordPress on your domain and your website will be live.

Similar to the process of setting up hosting, different providers have different steps for installing WordPress. However, most reputable hosts make it relatively simple to install with just a few clicks and a little bit of information.

In this book, we will be showing you how to install WordPress using cPanel. This will give you a good idea of the process. However, remember to refer to your provider's specific WordPress installation instructions.

In the screenshot below, you will see the cPanel interface and the section where you can install WordPress.

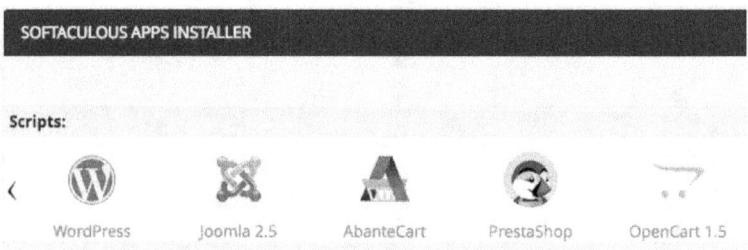

To start, select the WordPress icon.

This will open a new page, as shown:

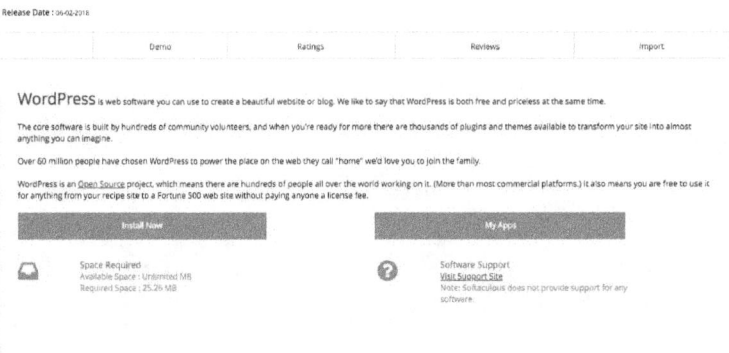

On this page, choose "Install Now." This will open another new page with a series of inputs for you to complete:

Software Setup	
Choose Protocol If your site has SSL, then please choose the HTTPS protocol.	https://
Choose Domain Please choose the domain to install the software.	adinfluence.com
In Directory The directory is relative to your domain and should not exist. e.g. To install at http://mydomain/dir/ just type dir. To install only in http://mydomain/ leave this empty.	wp

Site Settings	
Site Name	My Blog
Site Description	My WordPress Blog
Enable Multisite (WPMU)	☐

Admin Account	
Admin Username	admin
Admin Password	pass — Bad (18/100)
Admin Email	admin@adinfluence.com

Choose Language	
Select Language	English

Select Plugin(s)	
Limit Login Attempts (Loginizer)	☐

A few guidelines and tips to help you navigate this form:

- For the "In Directory" field under the "Software Setup" section, remove any text in that field. This ensures WordPress is installed on your root domain.

- Your site name (found under the "Site Settings" section) should be the same as your domain name without the .com extension. So, if your domain is "domain.com," your site name will be "Domain."

- You do not need to "Enable Multisite" (also found under "Site Settings"). This is generally only for advanced users or certain situations that do not apply to most online businesses.

- The "Admin Account" and "Choose Language" sections are fairly simple to navigate. Just enter a username and password that you will use for your WordPress login, enter the email address you want linked to your account, and select your preferred language.

- You can install additional security plugins, like the one that limits the amount of login attempts (so people cannot keep guessing your password until the get it). This is up to you and your security preferences.

- You don't need advanced options.

- Use the default theme provided. We will cover selecting a theme later in the process.

At the end of this form, you will need to choose an email address where your installation instructions sent. Follow these instructions to complete your WordPress installation. It should take no more than a few minutes.

You can now log in to your site with your username and password through your WordPress admin login page,

33

which you can find by typing in: yourdomain.com/wp-admin

Action Steps

- Click the WordPress icon on your host's interface to install.

- Fill out the relevant information, like site name, username, password, and email.

- After you finish the installation process, log in to your WordPress account to ensure that you have installed it correctly.

Tomorrow, you will go through the basic steps for setting up your site with WordPress.

Day Six: Set Up WordPress

Today, you will go through the basic steps of setting up your website. There are no frivolous extra steps at this point; every step today is important and vital. By the end of the day, you will have a functioning website for your online business!

Site Title And Tagline

The first thing you want to do is update your site title and tagline.

When you log into WordPress, you will be taken to the WordPress Dashboard, which will look something like this:

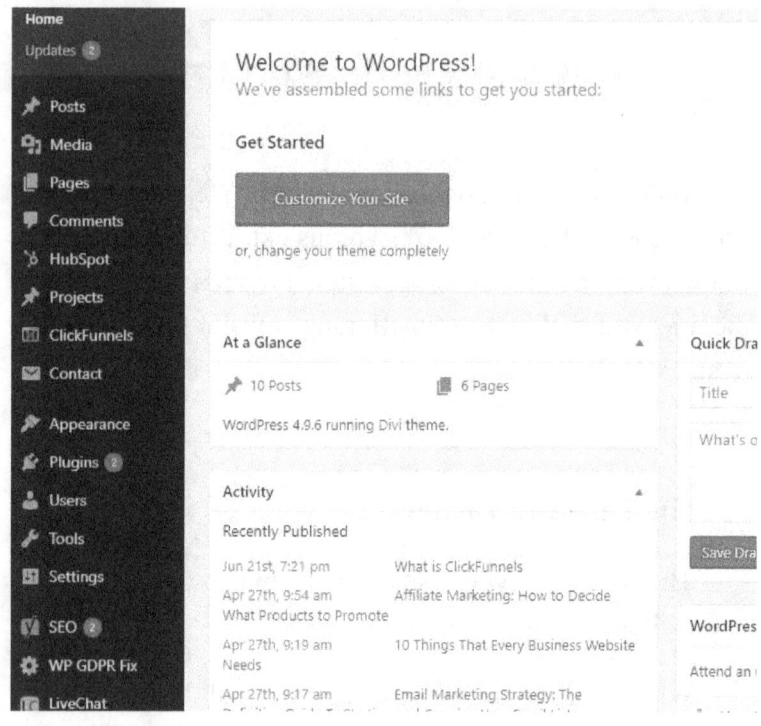

From there, scroll down and click on "Settings." This will take you to the "General Settings" page. You can also hover over "Settings" and choose "General" from the menu that pops up.

This page is where you can enter your site title and tagline:

General Settings

Site Title	Cute As A Button Clothing
Tagline	Kids' Clothing That's Cute As A Button
	In a few words, explain what this site is about.

Just ensure that your site title is the business/domain name you came up with. For the tagline, you can come up with a slogan or a short description that says more about what your online business does. You can even decide to leave this section blank, although I don't recommend that. When you've completed these sections, click on the "Save Changes" button at the bottom of the page.

Permalinks

Next, you want to update your WordPress permalinks. By default, WordPress displays page and post links as numbers. You can change the permalink structure for SEO and usability purposes. To do this, hover over "Settings" and choose "Permalinks" from the menu that pops up.

Choose the "Post Name" option, as shown:

Save your changes.

Delete Sample Content

When you install WordPress, it automatically adds sample content to your website. You should remove this sample content.

To find the content, hover over "Posts" on the WordPress dashboard and choose "All Posts" from the menu that pops up. This will show all posts on your website. You will most likely see a sample post titled "Hello World." You can remove this post by hovering over the title and clicking on the trash link that pops up. Then, hover over "Pages" on the WordPress dashboard and choose "All Pages" from the menu that pops up to find any sample pages WordPress may have created. Remove these by hovering over the title and clicking on the trash link when it pops up.

Create Foundational Pages

Next, you will create the foundational pages for your website. You are not yet concerned with the content that goes on these pages. At this point, you are simply creating the pages. You will create the content for those pages at a later date.

There are a few standard pages that most online business websites have. You can add any custom pages your particular business may need, but here is a list of those your website should have:

- Home
- Blog
- About
- Products
- Support
- Contact
- Legal

Menu

Once you create your pages, you need to create your navigational menu. To do this, hover over "Appearance" on the WordPress dashboard and choose "Menus" from the menu that pops up. You will see a page that looks something like this:

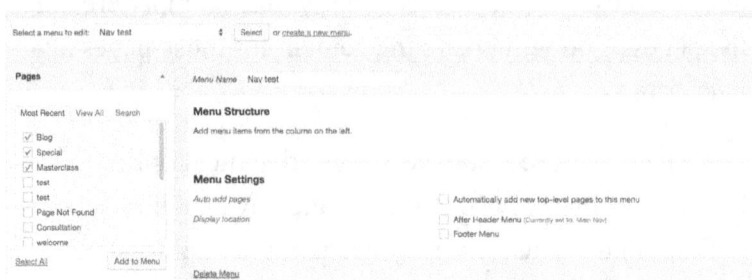

Click on "create a new menu," found at the top of the page.

Name your menu. Good choices are "Main Menu" or Main Nav."

Click "create menu."

Add the pages you created earlier to your menu by checking the box next to the page titles and then clicking "Add to Menu." You can then drag them around to reorder them.

A note for later: Once you have chosen your theme (tomorrow), you will need to set the location for your main menu under the "Manage Locations" tab. This will vary depending on the theme you choose.

Homepage And Blog Page

Next, you need to select which page you will use for your website's homepage and blog page. I know that you have already created a page called "Home" and a page called "Blog." However, these pages will not function as homepage and blog page until they are set as such. To do this, hover over "Setting" on the WordPress dashboard and choose "Reading" from the menu that pops up. You will see this at the top of the page:

Reading Settings

Your homepage displays
○ Your latest posts
● A static page (select below)

Homepage: — Select — ▼

Posts page: — Select — ▼

Ensure "A static page" is selected (as shown above). Then, select the page you created called "Home" from the Homepage field and select the page called "Blog" from the Posts page field.

Plugins

At this point, you are ready to pick plugins you want to use for your website. Plugins add additional functionality to WordPress. For example, the plugin "Contact Form 7" allows you to add contact forms to your posts and pages. You might want to install this plugin to add a form to your contact page.

Some of the most frequently used plugins are:

- Contact Form 7
- Askimet
- Yoast SEO
- W3 Total Cache
- Google Analytics For WordPress
- Wordfence Security
- Social Icons

You can explore these and many other plugins by choosing the "Plugin" tab on the WordPress dashboard. This page will list popular plugins and give you information and ratings about each one. Install any plugins you think you need. Later, you can add more plugins if needed.

Action Steps

- Update your site title and tagline.
- Update your permalinks.
- Remove sample content.
- Create your foundational pages.
- Create your website menu.
- Set your homepage and blog page.
- Install plugins.

Tomorrow, you choose a theme for your website and set up your website design.

Day Seven: Choose A Website Theme/Design

Today, you will be choosing the design of your website. Creating a great-looking WordPress website is actually pretty simple using professional themes, which is great because a fantastic website design can result in more leads and sales!

Finding A Theme

There are lots of places to find WordPress themes, but one of the easiest is right inside your WordPress dashboard. Hover over "Appearance" and choose "Themes" from the menu that pops up. You should see a number of themes you can pick from. You can also search for a specific type of theme you're after. For example, if your website is for Cute As A Button Clothing, you might search for "button" themes to find themes that incorporate buttons into their designs. Or, you might search for "whimsical" themes that match your focus on children's clothing.

For more features and arguably higher-quality designs, you can consider a paid theme from another source. Some of the top WordPress theme providers are:

https://www.elegantthemes.com/

https://www.studiopress.com/

https://themeforest.net/

There are many more, as well, if you are willing to go looking for them.

What Makes A Good Theme?

When selecting a theme for your website, you want to base your selection on a few factors, regardless of where you find it or how much it costs. Ask yourself if the theme:

1. will help you get more leads and sales.

2. is user-friendly to visitors.

3. is user-friendly to you, the admin.

4. works with your brand and brand message.

5. has the functionality that you need.

If you can check all these boxes, your theme is a winner!

Once you have selected your theme, you can make adjustments to the design to match your personal branding. For example, you can change the header background or link text color to one that matches your brand's color scheme. How and what you can adjust depends on the theme you have chosen, but whatever the theme, it should have tutorials available for changing the relevant factors.

Action Steps

- Choose a WordPress theme for your website.
- Go through the steps to set up your theme and personalize the design as needed.
- Browse your site to ensure everything is working and displaying properly.

Tomorrow, you will create a logo for your online business.

Day Eight: Create A Logo

You now have the bare bones of your website. Before you start to fill your pages with content, it's time to think about creating a logo for your online business. This will make your website seem much more professional and will automatically increase the quality perceptions of your products or services. By the end of the day, you will have (or be well on your way to having) a high-quality logo to put on your website.

Outsourcing

Your ability to create graphics will determine how you go about creating your online business's logo. If you have no graphic design skills whatsoever, it may be best for you to outsource the creation of your logo if it fits in your budget.

There are many services to which you can outsource this process. You may be able to find a graphic designer locally who will agree to design your logo for a reasonable price. You might prefer to search for a designer online. Here are a couple websites to get you started:

https://www.fiverr.com/

https://99designs.com

Each of these sites offers a range of prices and qualities when it comes to logo design. If you are just wanting something simple, you can always go the cheaper route and upgrade your logo as your online business flourishes.

Doing It Yourself

Another way to create your logo is the "do-it-yourself" option. Even if you can't create a logo from scratch by yourself, there are many places online where you can find logo templates to edit with a program like Photoshop. For example, Creative Market at https://creativemarket.com/templates/logos provides logo templates that you can purchase and customize for your business.

Another do-it-yourself option is to use a software tool like Canva at http://canva.com/. Canva is a free software tool for creating all kinds of graphics. The tool offers logo templates that you can download and edit. Many are free, but there is also a paid version for more options.

What Makes A Good Logo?

When creating your business logo, there are a few things to keep in mind:

- Choose a font and color scheme that match the feeling you want your business to have. Your logo is a visual representation of your business. Some colors and fonts have a specific feel to them. Some might feel elegant, feminine, futuristic, etc. Make sure the feeling people get from your logo represents the feeling you want them to get from your business.

- Try to make your logo memorable. A good logo sticks in people's memories. That's what you want. Create a logo that is both unique and easy to remember.

Incorporating Your Logo

Once your logo is created, go into Wordpress and add the logo to your website. Each WordPress theme has a different process for adding the logo. Refer to your theme's documentation to determine how to add or update your logo.

Action Steps

- Choose to either pay someone else to design your logo or create the logo yourself.

- Determine the feeling you want your logo and, by extension, your business to invoke in people.

- Create your logo and add it to your website.

Tomorrow, you will be creating the content for the foundational pages of your website.

Day Nine: Create Foundational Pages Content

Today, you will be creating the content for the foundational pages of your website. A few days ago, you created the foundational pages. Now, you will be adding the content to those pages. Specifically, you will be creating content for your legal pages, about page, support page, and contact page. We will discuss creating content for the blog and product pages you created later and in more detail.

At this point, you can also create some of the content for your website's homepage, but you might find that this is best left until you have completely finished the plan.

Legal Pages

Your legal pages are arguably some of the most important ones on your website, which is why you should create them first. They need to be easily accessible to your website's visitors and they should be reviewed by a lawyer to ensure all information is correct and everything is in order.

For quick and easy legal pages, you can use a tool like WP Legal Pages. You enter your business details and it will create the legal pages that you need. Remember to have these details checked by a lawyer.

After you have created your legal pages, you can include them in your website menu and your website footer on all pages of your website so that visitors can easily access them.

A good way to add them to your website menu is to create an item on your menu titled "Legal" and then make your legal pages a child to the parent "Legal." Basically, this means that when people hover their mouse over "Legal," your legal pages show up as clickable links.

About Page

The about page is one of the most-visited pages on most business websites! It is also one of the most overlooked and forgotten pages by website owners.

People want to buy from those that they know, like, and trust! That is why they often visit the about page. They want to learn more about the person they're buying from.

A great about page builds trust, connects you with your audience, and provides readers with the opportunity to join your email list or purchase the products you are promoting.

Most importantly, a great about page is more about your reader than it is about you! You want your about page to focus on your target audience and the problems you can solve for THEM.

For example, let's say your website helps people with Facebook ad campaigns. A great about page for this would start something like this:

Welcome to [WEBSITE NAME], where I help people just like you build amazing and successful Facebook ad campaigns.

Are you struggling to run profitable ads?

Are you sick of feeling like you're wasting your time and money?

Well, what if it didn't have to be so hard?

Imagine kicking off an ad campaign and seeing a return on investment and adding thousands of leads to your email list within just a few days..."

Notice how this about page intro is all about the potential customer and NOT the website owner.

Next, your about page can go into how your specific content can help them overcome the problems they're facing. You can do this by sending them to your blog, lead capture page, or products. You obviously have not filled all this content in yet, but you will do so in the next few days. For now, you can put in filler text.

Using the same Facebook ad campaign example, here is how you could transition into how you, specifically, can help them:

Does that sound too good to be true?

Well, it's not!

Here at [WEBSITE NAME], we have tons of free resources on our blog to get you started, like:

>> Title of blog post 1

>> Title of blog post 2

>> Title of blog post 3

And many more!

AND if you're ready to step it up a notch, you can check out our free mini-course on <u>The Ultimate Guide To Facebook Targeting.</u>

To find out more about how I can personally help you start earning massive returns on your Facebook ads, reach out to me through my contact page <u>here.</u>"

Notice the many solutions that were presented. They were given blog posts and a free mini-course to solve their problem. Then, if they wanted personal help, they could reach out directly. This is what your about page is all about: identifying your potential customers' problems and showing how you can solve them.

Support Page

Every website needs a support page. This page will be used by customers who have issues accessing products, who can't get their free downloads, who need to ask questions, or who have any other types of support requests.

For your support page, you can use a helpdesk tool like https://freshdesk.com/, a contact form plugin, or you can even just provide an email address for customers to email if they have issues.

If you decide to use the Contact Form 7 plugin recommended earlier, you can install a simple contact form that requires the customer to input their name, email, reason for request, and description of the issue. The form can be embedded right on your support page. When your customers submit the form, it is emailed directly to you. This is a simple but effective solution.

Contact Page

Your contact page should be an easy way for customers and potential customers to reach out to you. You can list your contact information (email, phone number, address, etc.) on your contact page or use a simple contact form like you did for your support page.

Action Steps

- Create the content for your legal pages.
- Create the content for your about page.
- Create the content for your support page.
- Create the content for your contact page.

Tomorrow, you will be setting up your online business's blog.

Day Ten: Set Up Your Blog

Today, you will be creating the blog for your online business's website. A blog is a major part of your online business because it serves as a hub for all of the free content you put out into the marketplace. This content generates leads and helps turn those leads to actual customers.

Another great thing about a blog is that it is an owned asset. When you put content on other platforms like Facebook or YouTube, your content is subject to the whims of those platforms. They can decide to delete your content at any time and should they shut down, your content is lost. Having your content on your own blog means that it is safe from these kinds of platform issues.

What Makes Good Content?

The content on your blog has a few primary purposes:

- Bring awareness to your business and what you offer.
- Turn traffic into followers and fans.
- Convert prospective customers into customers.
- Nurture and educate existing customers.

You should create strategic content that will help you achieve at least of the four objectives mentioned above. If it doesn't help you achieve any of these objectives, then you probably shouldn't be blogging about it.

Your First Post

For your first post, think about something specific which your customers are struggling. What is something you can cover that will help them with that specific problem?

Once you have an idea of what you want to cover, come up with an appealing title for your post. The goal is to address a topic they are interested in and make them curious about the post's content. For example, "The simple change you need to make to start losing weight" or "One big secret to getting more targeted eyes on your Facebook advertisements"

Next, outline the five to 10 main ideas you will cover in your post. These will become your post's headings, which you can use as a guide to write your content.

You can choose to either write your blog post inside the WordPress editor or do it in a word processor document and paste into WordPress later.

To get to your WordPress editor, hover over the "Posts" tab on the WordPress dashboard and choose "Add

New" from the menu that pops up. You will see a page like the one pictured below (minus the text in the fields).

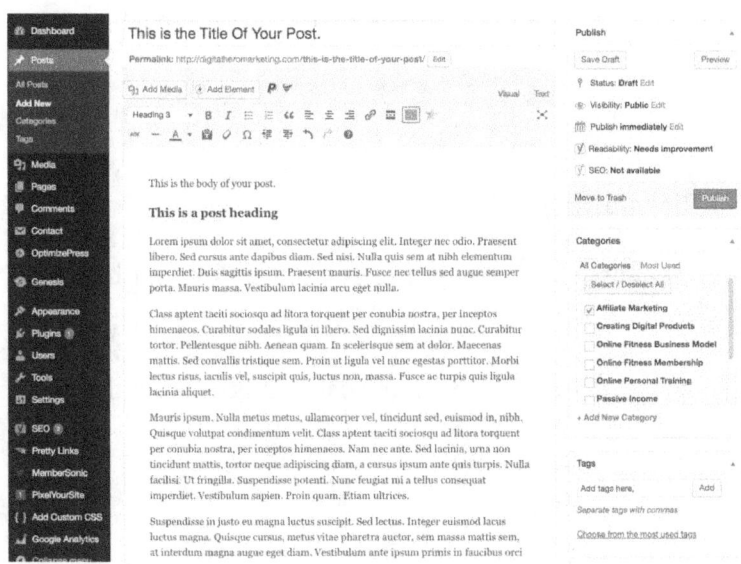

Enter your title in the post title section and enter your content in the body section. To add headings, click the dropdown box that says "Paragraph" and change to the heading style you prefer. In the example above, "Heading 3" was used.

Next, add relevant images to your post. Images make your posts more exciting and much easier to read. A good rule of thumb is to ensure there is always (part of) an image visible. In other words, every time your reader will have to scroll to read more, add an image.

Once your post is complete, select or add a category for your post and add relevant tags. You can also add featured images if your WordPress theme displays post images on your blog archive pages. This can make your blog look both more professional and more appealing to readers.

Formatting

Here are some formatting guidelines for your blog posts:

- Be sure to use white space and break up the text.
- Break your posts into sections with main points as headings.
- Use bold and italics to highlight important points.
- Break up the text with images.
- Use short paragraphs to improve readability.

Related Posts

Adding related posts is a great way to get people to consume more of your content. The more content they read, the more likely they are to buy your offers. You can add widgets to the sidebar for related posts or use plugins to add related posts to the bottom of each of your posts.

Optimizing Your Sidebar

Your sidebar is a great place to have a banner leading to your opt-in page, as well as banners for any products you are promoting. Your readers will be at different stages of the customer journey. Some will be existing customers, some will be prospective customers, and some will be traffic that is brand new to you. You want your blog to offer something for each of them, which is why you should have several banners on your sidebar.

Optimizing Your Blog Post Footer

After someone has consumed some of your content, they are primed to consume even more. That is why the footer is another great place to add a promotional banner for your opt-in page or one of your offers.

Optimizing Your Content

Don't forget about your blog content itself! As you write, find ways to include relevant links to your opt-in page, products, and services. For example, you can mention a client's story and share a link to learn more about your coaching.

Action Steps

- Come up with the idea and title for your first blog post.

- Outline the main ideas you will cover in your post.

- Add your content to the WordPress editor.

- Add images to your content.

- Format your content.

- Publish your first blog post.

- Add a widget or plugin to display related posts.

- Optimize your blog sidebar, footer, and content.

Tomorrow, you will be creating your free giveaway.

Day Eleven: Create A Free Giveaway

Today, you will be creating one of the most important assets you can have as an online business owner. A free giveaway will allow you to collect a database of leads in your autoresponder account to which you can mail your offers and promotions.

What Makes A Good Free Giveaway?

A good free giveaway is:

- **Irresistible.** People should just *have* to have what you are offering.

- **Specific.** Your free giveaway should solve one specific problem for your potential customer.

- **Easily consumed.** You don't want to be giving away a 300-page ebook or a two-hour-long video course. You want it to be something like a short PDF, action guide, cheat sheet, or video that can be consumed in 10 to 20 minutes tops.

A free giveaway should also:

- **Lead your prospective customers to your products and services.** Your free giveaway should educate and inspire your prospective customers to take the next step and make a purchase.

- **Deliver an end result.** The prospective customers downloading your free giveaway should get valuable information out of it that delivers results.

Types Of Free Giveaways

Action Guides

An action guide is a short PDF anywhere from three to 10 pages that gives actionable advice on achieving a very specific end result. For example, a personal trainer might give away an action guide on the top three ways to boost your metabolism and burn fat all day long.

Cheat Sheets

A cheat sheet can be as short as one page or slightly longer. Basically, a cheat sheet gives a series of steps to make a difficult process easier to follow. For example, there might be an "8-step cheat sheet to writing the perfect blog post."

Videos

A free giveaway video is almost like a cheat sheet or action guide in video format. It is typically a five to 15 minute long video that walks somebody through a specific process to get a specific result. Either of the examples given for the previous types of giveaways could be recorded as videos. If your target audience likes to consume more visual content, you may want to consider videos before other giveaway types.

Formatting

Once you have prepared your free giveaway, it is time to export it in its final format. For cheat sheets and action guides, PDF files are often the best choice. For videos, you can export them as .mp4 files.

Once exported, you will need to host your giveaway file online.

You can host PDFs right on your WordPress website. To do so, hover over the "Media" tab on your WordPress dashboard and select "Add New" from the menu that pops up. Next, click "Select Files" to browse your computer and upload the PDF file. After uploading, click "Edit" on the file and copy the file URL. This will give you the link that you can send to your new subscribers in a later step.

If your free giveaway is a video file, then you will want to use a third-party hosting platform like YouTube or Vimeo. A free option is to use YouTube and upload your video as "unlisted" so it doesn't show up in YouTube's search results (since you want people to subscribe to access the video). Once you have uploaded your video, you will need the embed code to later embed on your thank you page.

Action Steps

- Choose the type of free giveaway you want to create.

- Create your free giveaway content.

- Export it to its final format.

- Get the link or code you will need to add it to your thank you page.

Tomorrow, you will be setting up an autoresponder.

Day Twelve: Set Up An Autoresponder

Today, you will be setting up an autoresponder account so that you can capture leads and communicate with them via email. There are many different options for choosing an autoresponder. A few of the most popular autoresponder companies are:

https://www.aweber.com/

https://www.getresponse.com/

http://www.activecampaign.com/

https://mailchimp.com/

Basic Setup

Although each autoresponder will have a slightly different setup, they all work similarly and have similar setup processes. Generally, you will need to provide your name, your email address (the email address you want your autoresponses to come from), and your business address (for billing purposes). It is best to have your email address on the domain of your online business. So, if your domain is cuteasabuttonclothing.com, then your email might be yourname@cuteasabuttonclothing.com.

Lists

Once you have made it through the initial setup, you will need to set up your first email list. Lists are a way to organize subscribers. For example, you might have a different list for each free giveaway you have. Or, you might have different lists for buyers and free email subscribers. Splitting your subscribers into different groups like this is known as "segmenting."

For now, set up one new email list for the free giveaway that we will be covering tomorrow. As an example, we will create this new list in AWeber:

Click on the "Manage Lists" tab and then click on "Create A List," as shown:

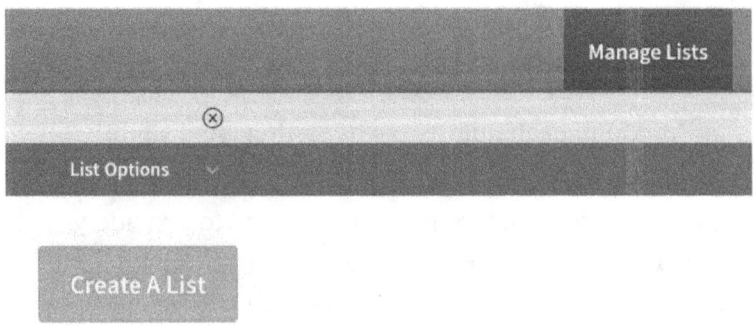

Next, fill in the details for your list:

A list is a group of subscribers who have given you permission to send them broadcasts (one-time messages and newsletters) or campaigns (automated series of messages) via email. Think of it as a group of people or contacts with common interests who want to hear from you.

Your Company Name

| Your company Name |

Your Company Website

| http://yourcompanywebsite.com |

What address would you like to include at the bottom of your emails? Explain This.

○ Use a different address

What sender name and email address should appear with your emails?

Sender Name

| Your Sender Name |

Sender Email

| Yourname@domainname.com |

[Next Step]

Then, name your list and give it a description:

What would you like to name your list?

List Name

[(Example) Weekly low fat recipes]

Briefly describe the emails your subscribers are going to receive.

List Description 0/400

[(Example) Healthy low fat recipes for every budget sent weekly!]

Your subscribers will see this description. Where?

[Go Back] [Next Step]

Simply name your list the name of your free giveaway. Your description can be something fairly simple. Just make sure it is accurate and as catchy as possible (since your subscribers will see it).

Finally, set up confirmation message settings:

A confirmation message can be sent to a new subscriber when they join your list. It asks for their permission to receive email from you.

By customizing the message your subscribers are more likely to confirm if you use this option. More Info.

Language
Choose a language for pre-approved subject lines and default message content.

[English ▼]

Subject line
Choose an approved subject line or request a custom one. This is your current subject line.

[Confirm your subscription. ▼]

Request a custom subject line

Message preview
This is the confirmation message your subscribers will receive when they sign up for your list.

> Please click the button below to confirm that you'd like to receive email from {!listname}.
>
> [Confirm my subscription]
>
> Thank you!
> {!company_name}

[Edit message content]

[Go Back] [Approve Message & Create List]

When you're finished, click "Approve Message & Create List."

If you want to turn confirmation messages off, go to "List options" and then "List settings." Next, click on "Confirmation message." Scroll down to "Confirmation message settings." Toggle the on/off button to off for "Send confirmation message for AWeber sign up forms." It should look like this:

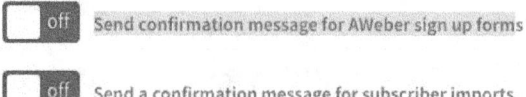

Autoresponder/Follow-Up Email Campaigns

Later you will be writing the email campaign for your online business. For now, let's briefly discuss what an autoresponder/follow-up email campaign is. In a nutshell, this is an automated series of emails sent to your subscribers after they join your email list. It is commonly used to deliver your free giveaway with the first email and then transition into a campaign that builds trust and promotes your products and offers.

Forms

Sign-up forms are put on your website to capture lead information. Most commonly, they are used to capture the names and email addresses of your subscribers. The tools you use to create your lead capture page will determine what you need to do to create your forms. This will be covered later.

Broadcasts

Broadcast emails let you send a real-time email out to all your subscribers at once. Unlike autoresponder emails that are prepared ahead of time, these emails are prepared and sent out as you want to contact your email list.

Action Steps

- Choose an autoresponder company.
- Fill in your basic account details.
- Set up an email address on your domain.
- Set up your first email list.

- Update your confirmation message settings.

Tomorrow, you will be setting up your lead capture page.

Day Thirteen: Set Up Your Lead Capture Page

Today, you will be setting up your lead capture page for your free giveaway. This page can also be referred to as a squeeze page or opt-in page and is arguably one of the most important aspects of your online business. Getting leads is essential to earning money and capturing those leads onto an email list is one of your biggest assets.

This means a couple of things:

- Your free giveaway has to be something that people want.

- Your lead capture page has to present your free giveaway in an enticing fashion so people want to download it.

There are different ways to write the copy for your lead capture page, but it's best to keep it simple. Two great formats are:

- Headline

- Form

- Button

and

- Headline
- Bullet Points
- Form
- Button

You can also add a visual representation, like an ebook cover or cheat sheet graphic, if it makes your offer more enticing.

Headline

Your headline is the second most important part of your lead capture page, as your giveaway offer itself is obviously the most important. Your headline should be specific and be focused on an end result.

A good example would be "Here Are The Top Three Ways To Boost Your Metabolism And Shed Unwanted Fat Fast!"

The end result: Get rid of unwanted fat.

Specifics: They are learning three ways to boost metabolism.

You should come up with 10 to 15 different headline variations for your offer before choosing your favorite. After that, you can add any elements from the other headlines you wrote to make it the best it can be. Writing your headline multiple times and multiple ways ensures that you come up with the best headline you possibly can.

Here is a variation of our example headline: "Get Rid Of Unwanted Fat Fast Using Three Simple Tips To Boost Your Metabolism." The concept is the same, but the wording is switched around.

After The Headline

If you are using the first variation of the lead capture page format, then you would place your form and button beneath the headline. If you are using the second variation of the format, you would come up with three to five bullet points that expand on what subscribers will get from your free giveaway.

Here are some bullet point prompts to help you come up with points:

The number one way to…

Exactly how to…

The single most important thing to…

The big secret to…

How to _____ without _____

The best way to…

My secret method to….

The easy way to…

Creating Your Lead Capture Page

Now that you have written your lead capture page copy, it is time to create the actual page on your site. The page-building tool you use will determine how you set it up. For example, you can integrate ClickFunnels with AWeber. After you integrate, it appears as a drop down in your integration settings and you simply select the list you want to add your subscribers to. You will want to refer to the specific instructions in your page-building tool and autoresponder for integration.

It is best to give your lead capture page an easy/memorable link on your website. It could be something like yourdomain.com/free-guide or yourdomain.com/3tips. Whatever you choose, make it short, easy to remember, and easy to give out over video or audio.

Action Steps

- Choose the format for your lead capture page.
- Come up with 10 to 15 headline variations.
- Choose your favorite variation.

- Analyze to see if you can further improve it.
- Add bullet points to the page if using them.
- Add your autoresponder form code to the page.
- Make the link easy to remember and give out.

Tomorrow, you will be creating the thank you page for your online business.

Day Fourteen: Create Your Thank You Page

Today, you will be creating your thank you page, another page that is key to your online business's success. It's the first page people see after subscribing to your email list to get your free giveaway and it is a valuable asset in building trust with your new leads. This means that it can also be a good place to make an offer immediately after someone subscribes. Leads who have already said yes once are likely to say yes again to the right offer, especially if this page delivers on your free giveaway promise like it should.

There are two basic ways to set up your thank you page:

1. Make the primary goal of the page to deliver the free giveaway and do a soft recommendation for your product or service.

2. Pitch your product or service and let your prospective customers know that they will be delivered the free giveaway content via email.

Way 1 builds more trust with a prospective client and can often lead to a higher long-term value per lead.

However, Way 2 often results in more initial sales and quicker profits.

Your goals will determine which method is best for your thank you page. If you are more interested in building a long-term sustainable business, however, I recommend that you go with the first option.

Now, let's break down how to create each page variation.

In Way 1, the page would follow a format like this:

Thank you for opting in! Access your free cheat sheet below:

[DOWNLOAD BUTTON]

[BANNER FOR AN OFFER]

This option immediately delivers on your free giveaway promise and builds trust.

Way 2 would be formatted like this:

Thank you for subscribing! Your free cheat sheet will be mailed to your inbox in the next five to 10 minutes, but first, please check out the special offer below:

[SALES COPY FOR YOUR OFFER]

[BUY BUTTON]

This option delays delivery of your free giveaway offer. It is likely that you will get more sales initially this way, but not necessarily in the long term.

Action Steps

- Choose to add either a soft recommendation offer or a direct offer to your thank you page.
- Create your thank you page copy.
- Make your thank you page live on your website.

Tomorrow, you will be choosing the core offer you will promote within your online business.

Day Fifteen: Choose Your Core Offer

Today, you will choose the core offer that you will be promoting for your online business. If you are unsure what this means, here's some explanation: You need one offer that is your primary focus. You should spend 90% of your time promoting this one offer and it should generate the majority of your income. By focusing on one core offer, you simplify your online business and can get better results and more conversions.

Your core offer can be your own product, coaching, or service, or it can be an offer that you promote as an affiliate. In any case, your core offer should:

- Solve a specific problem that your target market has.
- Provide a solution to that problem.
- Be priced competitively within the marketplace.

Deciding On An Offer

At this point, you need to determine what kind of core offer you want to promote. The goal is to choose something that you feel good about promoting and that you can seriously get behind.

You also want to think about your potential customers. What might they want? What result are they after? Is a product or a service that will be most helpful to them? Or is a course more likely to benefit them?

You also want to think about your goals. What do you need to charge per offer? How many do you need to sell? Think about these things before committing entirely to an idea.

Next on the agenda is to decide whether you will produce your own product or service or promote an affiliate offer. Each of these has both pros and cons and both are generally good choices. It is up to you to decide which is best for you.

Affiliate Offers

If you choose to promote an affiliate offer as your core offer, you want to make sure that it is a product that you like and that fits the criteria of a good offer. It is important that you see this offer as a valuable solution to the problem you are solving for your target market so that you can sell and promote it with confidence. It must be a product you are happy to promote. Customers will be able to tell if you do not have faith in the product!

With an affiliate offer, you also want to make sure it pays good commissions and the customers you refer are well supported. Even though you are not the product creator, you are recommending this product and therefore your reputation is on the line. You cannot afford to destroy the trust of customers by recommending a bad product (and you shouldn't want to recommend a bad product anyway).

Your Own Products And Services

Having your own products and services is great for your online business. One good thing about having your own products and services is that you keep 100% of the income generated from them. You are not only being paid a commission. Everything your products earn is yours.

You also have the added benefit of not sending your leads to someone else's customer list. When promoting an offer as an affiliate, you are sending your traffic to another vendor that then gets to keep the leads. Promoting your own products means building your own list of leads.

Action Steps

- Determine what kind of core offer you want to promote.

- Determine if you want to create your own offer or promote an affiliate offer.

Tomorrow, you will set up the sales engine for your core offer.

Day Sixteen: Set Up Your Core Offer Sales Funnel

Today, it is time to set up the sales funnel for your core offer. This will be the process that takes your leads and turns them into paying customers.

Choose Your Sales Funnel Method

There are a lot of ways to sell a product or service online. Some of the most common are:

- Sales letters
- Video sales letters
- Webinars
- And sales calls

If you are promoting an affiliate offer, there are other ways, like through:

- A bridge page
- An advertorial
- Or straight promotion

The method that you choose will be determined by the offer you're promoting and the price point of that offer.

For example, if you are selling a Facebook advertising services for $2,500 a month, it would be very difficult to sell that on a simple sales page. $2,500 is a lot of money for people to spend per month and they will most likely have a lot of questions. For a high price point and/or an offer that comes with lots of questions, you will most likely want to sell the service over the phone.

However, if you are selling a video course that comes with a one-time fee of $50, then a simple sales page or video sales letter will get the job done.

Maybe your offer falls somewhere in the middle of those two examples. Let's say you are selling a six-week course for $1,000. In this case, a sales page is too little, but you may not need to conduct business over the phone. A webinar may be the best solution.

What you need to do before choosing which method to use is conduct some research. What are others selling similar (and similarly-priced) products and services using? Are they selling via webinar, sales page, video sales letter, or phone? This will give you an idea of what you should be using, too.

Sales Funnels For Affiliate Offers

If your offer is an affiliate offer, then the vendor has already chosen and created one of those sales engine methods. Your goal is to sell prospective customers on the offer and get them to the vendor's sales funnel.

As mentioned earlier, there are a few ways you can do this.

You can send prospects to a bridge page. A bridge page is a page that typically includes a video of you talking about the affiliate offer, why they should get it, and how they can get it. Below the video, you can include a button that links to the vendor's sales page with your affiliate link. A bridge page is where you should offer your affiliate discount code (or other offer) if you have one.

A similar method is an advertorial. An advertorial is an article or blog post that delivers helpful content related to the affiliate offer and promotes the affiliate offer within the content. As with your bridge page video, the advertorial should tell the potential customer about the offer, why they should get it, and how they can get it.

A straight promotion for an affiliate offer is simply an email or something similar that has a very brief introduction to the product before sending the prospect straight to the sales page of the affiliate offer via your affiliate link.

Again, remember to do your research to decide which of these methods is best for the offer you are promoting (the vendor you are promoting may have some input here, so be sure to ask for their expert opinion).

Create Your Own Sales Funnel

Copywriting is a huge part of creating an effective sales engine. Regardless of the method you choose to use, copywriting plays a major role in conversions. You need to know what to say and how to say it.

When you are just starting out, the best way to create your sales engine is through a technique called "modeling." The idea is to find successful sales letters, video sales letters, or webinars to model.

Important: You are NOT copying the *content* of the examples you find. You will be modeling the *format* of these examples. How does each example move from section to section? How is the information broken up? By learning how successful examples are formatted, you can learn to format your content in a similarly successful way.

It is, interestingly, most effective to model a sales funnel for a product or service outside of your niche market. This will ensure that you are not modeling something in your niche and creating a presentation that is too similar. You SHOULD, however, look at the sales funnels employed by products similar to your own to see what works and what doesn't (and ensure you don't employ a method that doesn't work!).

Set Up Your Buy Buttons

The last component of setting up your sales funnel is setting up your buy buttons. There are many ways to take payments online, from standard PayPal buttons to cart software and affiliate networks. For simplicity, you can start out by creating a standard PayPal buy button. Instructions for doing this can be found directly from PayPal at https://developer.paypal.com/docs/classic/paypal-payments-standard/integration-guide/buy_now_step_1/

If you want more options, you can consider using a cart platform like https://www.stripe.com/ or https://thrivecart.com/ or https://www.samcart.com/

OR, if you want to use a cart platform that allows you to have affiliates, you can also consider http://warriorplus.com/ or https://www.jvzoo.com/

Once you are all set up with your platform of choice, you can get your button code and add it to your sales funnel page.

Action Steps

- Research your niche and find products similar to yours. How are they being sold?
- Choose your sales funnel method.

- Write your sales funnel copy. You can model this after a few examples.

- Set up your buy buttons.

Tomorrow, you will be writing your follow-up email campaign to promote your core offer!

Day Seventeen: Write Your Email Campaign

Today, you will be writing the email campaign for your online business. This email campaign will be used in your autoresponder follow-up campaign to promote your core offer.

A good email campaign will establish trust and turn prospective buyers into buyers. A typical follow-up email campaign is anywhere from seven to 21 emails and follows this general pattern (although there are no hard and fast rules):

- Day 1 — Welcome email and delivery of free giveaway offer.

- Days 2, 3, and 4 — Trust-building with relevant content.

- Day 5 and on — Helpful content with promotions for your core offer.

Day 1 — Welcome Email

Your welcome email delivers on the promise you made on your lead capture page. If you offered them a cheat sheet, you should include the download of that cheat sheet.

If you offered them free video content, you should send them the link to the page with that video content.

Depending on how you chose to set up your thank you page earlier, they may already have access to the free giveaway content. However, you should always send it in the welcome email as well in case something went wrong and they weren't able to access it.

You can also tell them in your welcome email how you can help them. You may even be able to get away with passively mentioning the programs your offer.

At the end of your welcome email, let your new subscribers know that over the next few days, you will be sending them valuable and relevant content.

Days 2, 3, And 4 — Trust-Building

The next three days of your email campaign will be used to further build trust with your new subscribers. A great way to do this is to deliver them tips and helpful information.

For example, if you're in the weight loss niche, you can send out a meal plan or some tips on the best exercises for weight loss.

Another way to build trust is to send them to content on your website. Maybe you have a video, podcast, or blog post where you shared some really valuable information and got a lot of positive feedback. You can send this to your new subscribers.

Day 5+ — Promotions

Next, your email campaign can transition to the promotion stage. You will start to focus on sending your new subscribers to your offer pages. The key to success is to mix it up. Sending the same promotional emails every day is not going to work. You need to look for multiple angles from which you can promote the product and generate interest.

For example, if you are promoting a weight loss course, one day you might talk about the importance of cardio exercises and recommend the product because it has an amazing cardio routine. Another day, you might discuss the necessity of healthy eating and promote the awesome meal plan that comes included in the course. Another day, you might promote the amazing testimonials from customers who have tried the course. And so on.

Be creative with your promotions and don't be afraid to mix in relevant content! You can even give your subscribers a taste of what you have on offer and leave them wanting more, which will prompt them to make a purchase.

For example, you could send a PDF of a one-week meal plan they can download. At the end of the PDF, let your subscribers know that the program you are promoting includes a 12-week meal plan.

Being creative and thinking outside the box like this will help you generate more sales!

Load Your Emails

Finally, load your emails into your autoresponder email campaign. There are conflicting views on the frequency with which you should send out your messages. Typically, anywhere between one to three days apart is a good bet.

Action Steps

- Write your welcome email.
- Write your trust-building content.
- Write your promotional emails.
- Load your emails into your autoresponder campaign.

Tomorrow, you will choose your authority platform.

Day Eighteen: Choose Your Authority Platform

Today, you will choose the platform you will use to create authority and drive traffic. There are lots of different platforms to choose from any many of them can help your online business grow in different ways. A few popular platforms are:

- YouTube
- Podcast
- Facebook
- Instagram
- Twitter

Each of these platforms has different merits. Do you need an extremely visual medium? You wouldn't want to choose a podcast then. Do you feel awkward in front of a camera? Then YouTube might not be for you. Do you like to write long, in-depth posts? Twitter probably isn't the way to go.

Choose a platform that will utilize your skills and that will work best for your specific niche. If you want, you can make a list of pros and cons for the top platforms. This might help you decide which is best.

Important: Do NOT try to use every channel at once. You need to choose one to focus on. If you try to start out making podcasts, videos, and posts for every platform, you will quickly find that you do not have enough time to devote to any of these endeavors. Your content will not be very high quality and you will not drive traffic back to your site.

Pick the one that works the best for you. Once you have, set up your business account. The requirements for this will vary based on the platform you choose. You might need to create a profile image, write a description, etc. Make sure you do a thorough job of this. Accounts with little information, no photos, or poorly-done setup will drive potential customers away.

Action Steps

- Pick your authority platform.
- Set up your account or profile.

Tomorrow, you will be creating the first pieces of content!

Day Nineteen: Create Your Content Base

Today is an exciting day, as you will be creating the first pieces of content for your authority platform and your website. By the end of the day, you will have five to 10 content pieces and you will be ready to start bringing in traffic and leads!

Create A List Of Ideas

The first thing you need to do is brainstorm a list of great content ideas. It's important to think about your core offer as you create this list and your content. This will ensure you are creating content that will attract the right people—those that want to buy what you are offering. You also need to think about your potential customers. What information are they looking for? What questions are they asking? You want your content to hold the answers they seek.

The next step is to go out and see what content they are already consuming. Search the platform you have chosen to use and see what kind of content exists in your niche. Who are the popular creators on your platform/in your niche? What type of content do they create? What content is getting the most views, likes, comments, and shares? What type of specific feedback are those content pieces getting? This will give you some insight into what is popular and what kind of information customers in your niche are looking for.

Go over your brainstorming list and your notes from research and make a list of five to 10 content pieces you will create. Then, create an outline for each piece of content. Once you have used these outlines to create your content, you can post them on your platform of choice and website. For example, if you record a video for YouTube, write a brief summary of that video and embed the video under the summary in a post on your blog.

Why bother doing this? You already have the video on YouTube! Remember that you want to continuously build your own assets even if you're using other platforms to build your audience. Think back to our discussion about platform regulations and shut-downs.

Action Steps

- Brainstorm content ideas.
- Research what content is popular in your niche and customers' reactions to it.
- Make a list of five to 10 content pieces you will create.
- Outline and then create your content.
- Post the content on your platform of choice.

- Post your content on your blog.

Tomorrow, you will be setting up retargeting pixels and a tracking system for your online business.

Day Twenty: Set Up Pixels And A Tracking System

You've almost reached the end of this guide! There are just a couple of days left until you have a fully-operational online business. Today, you will be setting up pixels and a tracking system.

What Are Pixels?

First of all, you might be wondering what "pixels" are referring to here. A pixel is a tiny graphic that is loaded when someone visits a website or opens an email, amongst other actions. The pixel can be used to track certain activities and are typically used to compile data for marketing purposes.

Platforms like Facebook and Google allow you to use pixels to build an audience for your ads. For example, you can use a pixel to track all the people who visit your sales page and do not make a purchase. Later, you can run a targeted ad campaign to those people to try and get them to buy. You could also put a pixel on your blog and run an ad campaign only targeting people that have viewed your blog. This is very valuable because your audience is already warm. Using methods like this can significantly increase your conversions.

Installing Pixels

How you install your pixels depends upon the network that you want to run your ad campaigns on. Let's use Facebook to demonstrate the process:

First, log in to Facebook. Then, go to the Ads Manager. If you do not have a Facebook advertising account, you will need to set that up first.

Once inside the Ads Manager, go to the menu. Under "Measure & Report," select "Pixels." Find the pixel that you want to use or create one if this is your first time. Then, click the setup button. Choose the option to manually install the code yourself and copy the pixel code to your clipboard.

Insert that code into the header of any page from which you want to capture an audience (for example, your lead capture page, your sales page, your blog, etc.). To do this in WordPress, you can use a WordPress plugin like http://www.pixelyoursite.com/

There is also a handy Chrome extension called Facebook Pixel Helper that will check and make sure your pixel is working on your site. It will tell you if a pixel is installed on the page you are viewing.

Set Up Tracking

Knowing what is working and what isn't working for your business is extremely important. You will want to know things like:

- Traffic numbers
- Conversion rate on your lead capture page
- Sales numbers
- Revenue generated
- Cost per lead
- Profit/loss

How you track your specific numbers will depend upon the systems you use. For example, ClickFunnels provides the majority of the information you need in one nice interface that looks like this:

Page Views		Opt-Ins	
All	Uniques	All	Rate
225	174	79	45.40%
107	78		
27	17		

You can also install Google Analytics or another tracking software. Once you have the information, you can use a simple Google Spreadsheet to track your numbers like this:

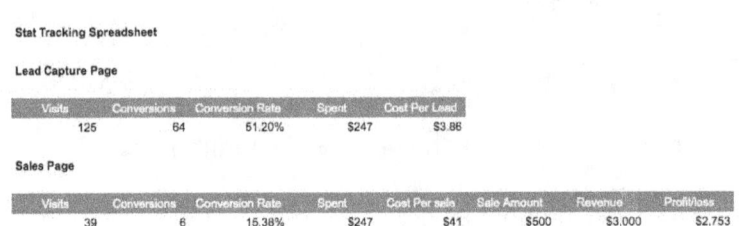

Having a system of tracking in place allows you to make adjustments, improve your conversions, and earn more with your online business! You should update your tracking spreadsheet on a daily basis and evaluate your figures weekly and monthly to implement necessary changes.

Action Steps

- Obtain your pixel code.

- Install a pixel WordPress plugin so you can add the code to your pages.

- Add the pixel code to the pages you choose.

- Set up a tracking spreadsheet.

- Monitor your figures and make adjustments as needed.

Tomorrow, you will be setting up your backend funnel.

Day Twenty-One: Set Up Your Backend Funnel

You have made it to the final day! Today, you will be setting up your backend funnel.

Have you ever heard the phrase "Money is made on the backend?"

While that may not always be true, there is certainly MORE money to be made on the backend. Your backend funnel should consist of one or more offers that you promote aside from your core offer, which will allow you to maximize lifetime customer value and earn more money in the long run.

How To Set Up Your Backend Funnel

Your backend offers should fall into one of two categories:

1. Help the customers on a deeper level than is provided by your core offer.

2. Offer something related to but different from your core offer.

As an example, if your core offer is a video course for teaching photographers how to shoot the perfect wedding photographs, then a backend offer could be a six-week one-on-one coaching package. The coaching package would allow you to work with them at a deeper level and better answer their questions.

Plan out one or a few offers that you will put in your backend funnel. You can then set up a sales engine and an email campaign for your backend offers just like you did for your core offer.

Action Steps

- Choose the type of offers you will add to your backend.

- Create the sales engine for your backend offers.

- Create the email campaign for your backend offers.

Final Words

Congratulations! You have made it through all the steps and are now ready to launch your online business! You have done a lot of work over the past 21 days, but this is only the beginning. It is now time to take your business to the next level by following your plan of action and meeting the goals you set early on. With this game plan, you have laid a solid foundation on which to build a successful online business!

Visit www.OnlineBusinessGamePlan.com/bonus for exclusive extra bonuses.

www.ingramcontent.com/pod-product-compliance
Lightning Source LLC
Chambersburg PA
CBHW070659220526
45466CB00001B/506